Original title:
Ferns by the Fireplace

Copyright © 2025 Creative Arts Management OÜ
All rights reserved.

Author: Benjamin Caldwell
ISBN HARDBACK: 978-1-80581-945-5
ISBN PAPERBACK: 978-1-80581-472-6
ISBN EBOOK: 978-1-80581-945-5

Fernaceous Refuge from Winter

In the corner, green things sway,
Looking cozy, come what may.
Hot cocoa spills, a comic brew,
A leaf drops down, in giggles too.

The cat jumps high to claim a right,
Thinks he's stealthy, feels so slight.
Foliage chuckles, acting sly,
"Just when will he learn to fly?"

Through the chill, a warmth we gain,
With silly dances, we entertain.
Mismatched socks make us all beam,
While shadows twirl in a wacky dream.

Amidst Laughter and Greenery's Light

Green webs hang like twisted jokes,
While we sip tea and poke fun at folks.
Laughter erupts, a burst of glee,
"Is that a plant, or a friendly bee?"

The pots are filled with tales untold,
Whispers of summer, bright and bold.
A dance-off planned, with plants as judges,
We twirl and spin, avoiding grudges.

Steam from the kettle plays a tune,
As the daisies sway, a merry croon.
Silly hats atop our heads,
Wearing laughter like festive threads.

Tranquil Shadows Dancing by the Hearth

In twinkling light, shadows prance,
Hilarity arises as we chance.
A pot of soup, splashes galore,
"I swear it's soup, not a nature war!"

Glow of embers, jokes take flight,
As plants wear hats, quite a sight!
Branches swing, a concert starts,
With giggles fluttering in our hearts.

Every rustle, a secret sigh,
In this haven, we laugh and try.
With knick-knacks shaking, we find delight,
Under the warmth, all feels so right.

Whispers in the Hearthlight

In the nook, where the shadows play,
A plant winks, like it's got something to say.
It fluffs its leaves with a cheeky grin,
"Do I look cozy? Come sit, join in!"

The logs crackle, the embers dance,
Our leafy friend dreams of a prance.
"Just look at me, I'm quite the sight,
Who needs a candle? I'm the real light!"

Green Shadows in the Glow

In the corner, a leafy sage,
With secrets to tell, loud and age.
"Forget the romance; I'm here for the cheer!
Look at me thrive when the winter is near!"

Who knew a sprout could be so bold,
Sharing such tales in the warmth of the gold?
With giggles and rustles, throughout the night,
Our friend gives a wink, and all feels right.

Lush Echoes of the Flame

Among the cushions, it takes a stand,
Full of mischief, it stretches its hand.
"Why sit so close? You're risking the heat!
Don't roast yourself; have a seat, have a seat!"

As if in a play, it sways with glee,
Making us laugh with its leafy decree.
"Join me for stories; trust me, it's fun,
I'm the life of the party, when days come undone!"

Verdant Dreams Amidst the Ember

In a pot so round, it loves to boast,
About wild adventures, it's done the most.
"Just yesterday, I met a rolling pine,
We shared some giggles over elder wine!"

And as the heat wraps us in embrace,
Our leafy hero's got the perfect place.
With a chuckle, it whispers, "How about some fun?
Let's turn this night into a rhyming run!"

Fronds and Flickers

In cozy nooks, the gremlins play,
Furry fronds flirt as shadows sway.
A warm glow whispers, 'Who's that near?'
Just furry friends, no need to fear!

The cat joins in with a cheeky grin,
As leaves do a jig, and we all spin.
Hot cocoa spills, a sweet delight,
With frothy mustaches, we laugh in the night!

Secrets Wrapped in Hearthwarmth

The quiet glow holds secrets tight,
As ferns plot mischief in the night.
They giggle low, while branches twist,
Conspiring plans in a green mist.

'This is our time!' the ivy shrieks,
As giggly ferns share saucy sneaks.
A marshmallow roast turns to a fight,
With sticky fingers and laughter bright!

Sylvan Shadows Danced in Light

Shadows shimmy, a leafy waltz,
Rooted talents hide their faults.
Leafy dancers, bold and sleek,
In our living room, they peek.

Laughter echoes, a playful tune,
As spores take flight beneath the moon.
With every flicker, they sway and sway,
Plant mischief-makers on display!

Nature's Embrace by the Fire

In this nook, the world retreats,
Fungal friends on cushioned seats.
Laughter bursts, as we unwind,
Nature's tricks are well-designed.

The embers pop, a secret club,
While leafy jesters move and rub.
'Who's got the s'mores?' a voice does scream,
With gooey treats, we live the dream!

Ember's Kiss on Leafy Dreams

The leaves are plotting, oh what fun,
With embers dancing, they've begun.
Giggles of greens, in a bubbly way,
Wishing for a ride on their fiery ballet.

At night they twinkle, a leafy crew,
Crafting schemes of what they'll do.
A cozy laugh among the glows,
Who knew leaves could be such pros?

The Retreat of Green in Warmth

The greens all gather, snug and bright,
Beneath the warmth, a whimsical sight.
Chasing shadows while sipping tea,
Green giggles float like bumblebees.

They slip and slide, a comical spree,
Plotting mischief, oh, can't you see?
In cozy corners, they share a toast,
To the warm glow, they love the most.

Hearth Emotions and the Lush Undergrowth

Among the flickers, nerves do tingle,
While greens do plot, a messy jingle.
With a twinkle here and a snicker there,
A collective smirk fills the evening air.

Fluffy cushions, under leaves they crawl,
Creating a ruckus, having a ball.
Who knew greens could dance and sway?
Crackling laughter fills the fray.

Serenity of the Green Shadows

In shadows where the green things play,
They whisper tales in a jolly way.
The crackle, pop, a twinkle of mirth,
Who said plants can't have fun on earth?

Whimsical whispers of crinkled leaves,
Sharing jokes that no one believes.
In the twilight glow, their joy does bloom,
A leafy party in the living room!

Hearts of the Hearth in Verdant Glow

In a corner, green and bright,
Leaves tell tales of cozy night.
A plant that dances, sways with glee,
Oh, what a friend you are to me.

Laughter bursts like crackling fire,
You wink at me, you never tire.
In your shade, I seek my snack,
Adventures wait, no need to track.

The flicker jumps, you shimmy close,
Offering warmth, a leafy dose.
My wooden chair starts to recline,
With every sip, life feels divine.

So here we sit, your fronds so grand,
Together crafting mischief, planned.
In this nook, we spread our cheer,
Who needs the world when you're right here?

Embracing Nature in a Flickering Refuge

A wriggly worm made quite a scare,
Danced past the flames without a care.
A leafy friend was standing by,
Said, "Don't fret; just watch it fly!"

Underneath the twinkling spark,
We plotted pranks till it got dark.
With each crackle, we shared a joke,
And I hid behind my leafy cloak.

The shadows bobbed, they wiggled tight,
As ferns groaned softly with delight.
Hot cocoa flew and laughter reigned,
What a spectacle, everyone gained!

So in this nook of flick'ring light,
We celebrate the silliest sight.
You, my green and trusty mate,
Make this refuge truly great!

Soft Ferns and the Fire's Breath

The fire crackles, sparks ascend,
Green leaves chuckle, they pretend.
"We're lucky here, just take a seat!",
They tease my toes, so warm and neat.

I'd tell a joke, but they might leaf,
With every pun, it's sheer belief.
A blaze of giggles fills the air,
While frolicking fronds are everywhere.

Hot marshmallows out of reach,
You tease me with your leafy speech.
"Just stretch a little! Join the fun!"
Together we will always run.

So play along, soft leafed friends,
In our sanctuary, laughter bends.
With every flicker, tales are spun,
Under this glow, we are all one!

Refuge of Shadows and Hearthlight

In shadows cast from fire's light,
A leafy prankster starts to bite.
Its gentle tease, a tug on me,
"Come closer now, just wait and see!"

The embers' dance, the ferns repeat,
With every laugh, the fun's replete.
Bright-eyed mischief warms the air,
For every glance, I find you there.

The crackle tells a secret sound,
Nature's riddle that knows no bound.
With whispers shared, we jump and sway,
No boring "how are you?" today!

So here's to warmth and leafy cheer,
We conquer shadows, have no fear.
Together in this cozy nook,
You, my friend, have got the hook!

Hearthbound Secrets of the Woodlands

In the corner, a plant did cheer,
Hiding secrets, oh so dear.
A squirrel peeked in with a grin,
Wondering what mischief might begin.

The cat thought it was a new friend,
Curled up close with no intent to fend.
The plant waved back with all its might,
"Just passing time, no need to bite!"

A spark flew out and caused a dance,
A mushroom jumped, oh what a prance!
The room erupted in laughter and joy,
Even the dust bunnies joined the ploy!

Tales of woodland fables shared,
With warmth and whimsy—nothing bared.
The fireplace listened, crackling keen,
While plants giggled at this unseen scene.

Vitality in the Warmth of Glow

A lively green in glowing light,
Danced around, full of delight.
"Do you know the latest news?"
Asked the leaf, avoiding blues.

The flame popped loud, an audience near,
"Tell us quick, we've much to hear!"
With stories of woodland pranks so bold,
They laughed together till the night grew cold.

A friendly log chimed in with flair,
"Did you hear about the bear in my chair?"
A chuckle echoed from the hearth,
As all celebrated this time of mirth.

With giggles that rang like sweet chimes,
Leaves in laughter forgot their climes.
And glow from embers lit the night,
Magnificent mischief, what a sight!

Whispers of Green in Ember's Glow

In the shadows, whispers played,
Green wonders on parade.
A frond flicked its tips in jest,
Challenging a log to a leafy fest.

The fire chuckled, a teasing spark,
What antics brewed in the dark?
The green laughed back, a leafy tease,
"Keep it quiet, or I may freeze!"

Suddenly, a beetle rolled in,
Declaring loudly, "Let's begin!"
With a wink from the glow so bright,
They planned to frolic through the night.

One by one, the hearth did fill,
With ferns and giggles and all their will.
The fireplace watched, an amused spectator,
As plants turned into lively creators.

Lush Leaves and Flickering Flames

Leaves debated which could dance best,
Challenging flames for a silly quest.
"Bet you can't wave without a flick!"
"Hold my water, I'll do the trick!"

The flames bounced back with fiery pride,
"Just watch us twirl, we won't hide!"
As laughter spun in the air so sweet,
A match lit up, oh what a treat!

With quirky twirls and foxtrot flair,
The green took off, without a care.
"Come join us, flames, it's a jolly show!"
And so they giggled, putting on a glow.

In this warmth, delight took flight,
Woodland whispers brightening the night.
A comedy on this cozy stage,
Where leaves and flames turned the page!

Gentle Shadows at the Flame's Picking

As shadows dance with glee,
The flames twist and twirl,
A fern with funny flair,
It thinks it's quite the whirl.

It nods to the crackling sound,
A leaf with such delight,
It wave its fronds around,
In this cozy, warm night.

The cat leaps with sudden surprise,
At shapes that flicker and fly,
With a hop and a joyful pounce,
It joins the leafy high.

The laughter of friends will ring,
As we sip our mugs so warm,
To the ferns and the silly things,
That comfort keeps us from harm.

Embraced by Warmth and Verdant Dreams

In a corner, green they sway,
Tenacious little things,
They laugh at the fire's display,
As joy like music rings.

A leaf almost takes a bow,
In the warmth of the blaze,
It's the star of the show now,
In this glow, it plays.

Beside the logs all stacked and neat,
A quick wit shines so bright,
Chatting up the heat,
What a glorious sight!

So let the stories be told,
With the ferns joining in,
Cackles will soon unfold,
In this mirthful din.

Echoes of Green in Flickering Dusk

Flickering light from the blaze,
Sparks do a funny jig,
Greens giggle in a haze,
As they play hopscotch with a twig.

The coffee pot whistles loud,
While leaves glimmer with glee,
In this leafy, playful crowd,
They're all wanting to be free.

One frond whispers a little joke,
About mushrooms dressed in hats,
As laughter slips like smoke,
The cat gives him some spats.

The air is ripe with cheer,
And the warmth feels just right,
Joy echoes from ear to ear,
In the cozy, soft night.

The Warmth of a Cozy Forest

Under the glow, leaves convene,
A swirl of green, a playful bunch,
With humor woven in between,
And jokes that make a punch.

The fireblower is quite a show,
As embers dance up high,
While greens engage in a row,
And challenge the open sky.

A game of tag ensues,
As the flames flicker low,
Laughter gives them all the cues,
To two-step in the glow.

They plot and plan all night,
In whispers soft and sly,
For a grand leaf-rocket flight,
In this warm and merry sky.

Hearth's Gentle Guardians

In a corner, leafy friends sway,
Keeping warmth at bay, hooray!
With each crackle, they seem to grin,
Whispering tales of where they've been.

A couch potato's cushy reign,
While they dance, he feels no pain.
A cozy spot, a soft retreat,
Their laughter echoes, oh so sweet.

The Ferns' Vigil by the Flame

Watching closely, they never blink,
Judging popcorn with a wink.
Each flicker makes them sway and cheer,
"Is that a snack I see, oh dear?"

With every joke around the fire,
They glow with leafy, leafy desire.
Keeping secrets, oh so spry,
In their verdant, leafy high.

Nature's Canvas Toasting in Radiance

A canvas of green in glowing light,
As the flames dance and take to flight.
Artistry done, with no brush,
They'd paint a laugh in a leafy hush.

"Can we roast marshmallows?" one does dare,
While others ponder, "Can we share?"
With crackled laughter, the leaves do sway,
Banishing dreariness, come what may.

Hearthlight Dreams of the Green

In dreams, they leap with glee and flair,
Searching for snacks with a leafy air.
Who knew green could be so bright?
Sharing giggles all through the night.

A leafy crowd with perfect skin,
Holding court, they wear a grin.
"Who's for more laughs?" one can hear,
Toasting dreams with hearty cheer.

Enchanted Leaves in Dappled Light

In the corner grows a plant,
With leaves that seem to chant.
They wiggle and they wave so free,
Wonder what they see from me?

A critter poses, strikes a pose,
I swear it's plotting some grand prose.
Dappled light tricks the eye somewhat,
Is that a leaf, or a roaming brat?

Mossy feet and laughter too,
This little squad, a leafy crew.
Their fashion sense cannot be beat,
In nature's dance, they bring the heat!

So let's toast to these leafy pals,
Rattling with giggles, sprightly yowls.
Around the hearth, they throw a ball,
Those lively greens, they're quite the thrall!

Whispered Secrets in the Hearth's Twin

Gather round, the fire's bright,
Green spies whispering at night.
No one knows just what they say,
But I suspect they're here to play!

With wobbly legs, they dance around,
In leafy flaps, they dominate the ground.
Is that a wink from one to me?
Or just a bug, oh dear, we'll see!

Twists and turns, such silly games,
All the plants have quirky names.
"Fluffy Bouncer" and "Wiggly Fred,"
They skip and giggle, never dread!

So don't fret, just grab some chips,
Join the fun with silly quips.
The fire crackles, laughter streams,
These green mischief-makers reign in dreams!

Gentle Ferns in the Warmth of Amber

In plushy warmth, they start to sway,
Gentle greens in laughter play.
A little fern with a wobbly frown,
"Who knew plants could wear a crown?"

With a nod and a gentle spin,
They chatter 'bout the dustbin kin.
One tells tales of raindrops sweet,
While another taps his leafy feet.

Unexpected quirks, they love to share,
Like how they caught a squirrel's hair.
Or staged a drama with the cat,
A leafy sequel, imagine that!

"Cheerio!" they cheer, then strike a pose,
Who knew plants had such high prose?
Gather 'round for giggles and fun,
Our cozy nook, a leafy pun!

Green Symphony in a Cozy Nook

In a nook where it's snug and tight,
Leaves are tuning for the night.
A green band starts its playful song,
With laughter bubbling all night long.

"Here, here!" calls the bravest sprout,
"Dance along! There's no doubt!"
Tiny whispers, a leaf's duet,
Jokers of green, the best you'll met.

With jazz hands made of silky green,
They bust a move, oh what a scene!
The fern brigade flaunts silly styles,
They break the silence with leafy smiles!

As the tune plays soft and low,
Bring your snacks, it's time to go!
Green symphony in a cozy nook,
Who wouldn't trade a glance or look?

Frond-Laden Comforts on Winter Nights

In the corner by the glow,
Green fronds flutter, putting on a show.
They wave to the logs, a leafy cheer,
Not caring if it gets a bit too near.

The cat leaps up with a bound,
Swatting at leaves, oh what a sound!
As twigs crackle in the bright array,
Our antics make the chilly fade away.

With each warmth a chuckle brews,
As the plants plot mischief from their views.
A cozy scene, but laughter's the best,
When the silly plants start a leafy fest!

So let the winter wind blow about,
We'll dance and prance, and laugh out loud.
For in this nook of warmth and delight,
The fronds and fun take flight tonight.

Secrets of the Hearth's Embrace

By the fire's glow, secrets are shared,
With fronds whispering tales, they never cared.
'The heat's too much!' they giggle and tease,
While glistened leaves sway as they please.

The old cat snores, oblivious to the plot,
As ferns spin stories, the best ones are hot.
'Last week we were giants!' one leaf did say,
While others rolled over to join in the play.

Mischief brews in a wintertime haze,
As we toss popcorn, hear the plants' praise.
They reach for the kernels, it's quite the sight,
Bouncing and dancing into the night.

So laughter erupts among those who stay,
Two-legged and green in a spirited way.
In the hearth's embrace, warmth now ignites,
With plants in a giggle, winter's just right.

Nature's Pulse in the Firelight

In the crackling warmth, the pulse we find,
With leafy companions, we're intertwined.
Little shadows dance, and we grin wide,
As the flickering light takes us for a ride.

They stretch and yawn, those playful fronds,
Waltzing along to the fire's soft songs.
'This heat's no bother!' one boldly claimed,\nWhile the
other fired back, 'You're just too famed!'

A teapot whistles, high-pitched and clear,
The plants gossip softly, we perk up to hear.
'Is that a new brew or the same old cup?'
They chortle and giggle, filling the cup up.

With laughter and warmth, the night rolls on,
Each moment cherished, till the light is gone.
Nature's pulse thrums in a comical show,
The firelight's magic! Oh, how we glow!

Ferns in the Hush of Candlelight

In the still of the night, beneath soft lights,
Whispers of greens spin in giggling flights.
They sway with glee, tickled by the glow,
As shadows dance playfully, high and low.

Candle flames flicker, secrets are told,
As leaves trade jokes that never get old.
'Watch your head!' cries one in a mock fright,
'That branch will trip you if you take flight!'

The warmth wraps gently, like a friend's embrace,
As the plants hold court in this cozy space.
Giggles flutter about like a soft breeze,
While moments like these are sure to please.

So raise a tea cup to this leafy cheer,
For in candlelight, all worries disappear.
Laughter's the soundtrack of this night spent,
With fronds in the hush, joy is the intent.

Coziness Between the Canopy

Amidst the cozy haze, they sway,
A leafy crowd, all here to play.
One's doing yoga, others just chill,
Who knew that greens had such a thrill?

Watch them gossip, give a little sigh,
"Did you see the squirrel? Oh my, oh my!"
Tangled up in a blanket, just right,
They laugh about their newfound height.

Hot cocoa spills, a fernish delight,
"Oops, I think I've sprouted!"—oh, what a sight!
The cat joins in, a fuzzy little star,
They all agree he's the best by far!

So here they gather, snug and spry,
With sips and giggles, they lift the sky.
A quirky crew of the greenest hues,
Who knew that plants could refuse to snooze?

Ferns' Solstice by the Fire

Gather 'round, the warm flames dance,
The greens chuckle, caught in a trance.
"Who put the marshmallows way up high?"
Said one to the other, with a snicker and sigh.

A toast to the light, so cozy and bright,
But what's with the shadows, oh what a fright!
One leaf teases, "I'm ready to grow!"
While the others roll eyes, all in a row.

With giggles and warmth, they pass the snack,
One sneezes; oh no! The laughter's on track.
"We're leafy and lovely, but quite a lot green,
Let's not serve salad, that's just too mean!"

As the stars twinkle, they share their stories,
Of forest adventures and fabled glories.
Under the moonlight, they sway with ease,
A festival of greens, beneath the trees.

Shadows of the Forest in the Hearth

The fire crackles, shadows twirl,
Leaves giggle, what a whirl!
"Did you just hear a ghostly shriek?"
Nervous yet raucous, they play hide and seek.

One green claims, "I was born to shine!"
While another quips, "You're always just fine!"
They dance 'round the warmth with whimsical flair,
Avoiding the cat, who gives them a stare.

A joke erupts, it's fern-fectly clear,
As they reminisce on their favorite beer.
"A stout for the roots and a pale for the zest,
We raise our cups high—here's to the best!"

With the hills outside covered in snow,
This leafy saga continues to grow.
Giggling and swaying, they bask till it's late,
In nature's embrace, they truly create.

Warmth Among the Whispering Greens

Chill in the air, but oh what a scene,
A gathering of sprouts, most lively and green.
One cracks a joke about photosynthesis,
While another responds with a leafy bliss.

The logs pop and crackle, with laughter they cheer,
"Who's turning crispy? It's getting too near!"
A leafy dance-off breaks out with glee,
"Last one to flop is a tree-bound flea!"

Tales of the woods wilder than any flight,
Whispered in whispers beneath the moonlight.
So long as we're cozy and laughter's a-mound,
In a riot of greens, joy can be found.

With cups of warm herbal, they toast to the night,
Their shadows are dancing, what a delightful sight!
In this snug little nook, they relish the fun,
A happy green party—oh, isn't it spun?

Serene Fronds Dancing with Firelight

In cozy nooks where embers gleam,
The fronds sway softly, it's like a dream.
They giggle as they watch the blaze,
Dancing shadows in a playful maze.

One little leaf gets too close to the heat,
Yells, "I'm crispy!" as it jumps to its feet.
The friends all laugh, their laughter so bright,
Creating a chorus in the warm, soft light.

While wood logs crackle with ancient sighs,
The green crew plots and schemes their surprise.
With tiny tips, they poke at the flames,
"Let's roast some marshmallows, or play funny games!"

As bedtime draws near, the shadows grow long,
The fronds whisper secrets, a leafy song.
With smiles on their faces, they snuggle up tight,
Ready for dreams in the soft, glowing night.

A Fire's Embrace for Woodland Spirits

The woodland crew comes to have some fun,
With a flick of the wrist, they dance, one by one.
Mossy little feet shuffle and glide,
With giggles and squeals, they cannot hide.

A tiny sprite flings a log in the air,
"Catch me if you can!" with a wild flair.
The flames flicker wildly, "I'm fire, be wary!"
But the spirits just chuckle, "You're not very scary!"

Crackles and pops echo through the night,
As twinkling stars wink in delight.
With leafy hats and twirl of the dust,
They may be fronds, but they're full of gusto and trust.

The fire's warm glow tells tales so bright,
Of woodland wonders wrapped in pure light.
With every cackle and radiant grin,
Even the fire knows it can't help but join in.

Twilight's Glow on Gentle Green

The glow of twilight wraps around the room,
As gentle fronds sway, dispelling the gloom.
With whispers so low, they share little jokes,
"Look at that log, it's dancing like folks!"

A firefly joins, lighting up the scene,
"Have you seen my tiny dance? It's quite a routine!"
The fronds all chuckle, waving back their cheer,
As glowing embers light the fun atmosphere.

Some leaves start to argue who's the best dancer,
While the fire rolls its eyes at the leafy romancer.
"Come on, you lot, you're all so spry!
Let's show the world a grand dance to the sky!"

So twirls and spins go on all around,
Till a gust of wind tumbles them down to the ground.
With laughter resounding, they all take a bow,
In the warm glow of night, here's the best fun of now!

Flickering Flames and Verdant Dreams

Flickering flames with a mischievous wink,
Make shadows dance, and make fronds rethink.
A dandelion sneezes, "I think I'll take flight!"
While ivy shouts back, "You'll land in the night!"

The fire's bright glow casts a shimmering spell,
As every little leaf shares a secret to tell.
"Who dared make s'mores without us here?"
As they plot and they scheme, it's all filled with cheer.

In a moment of fun, the glow starts to fade,
As drowsy fronds yawn, it's time for parade.
"Tomorrow's shenanigans will surely delight,
With stories to tell of our firelit night!"

So they curl up tight, in a soft leafy heap,
As the crackling wood whispers them off to sleep.
In dreams made of laughter and sparks that ignite,
They'll keep the adventure going through the night.

Nature's Lullaby Cradled in Warmth

In the nook by the fire, there's a leafy surprise,
A dance of green fronds, with humor in their guise.
They sway and they wiggle, oh what a delight,
As embers crackle softly through the cozy night.

The warmth wraps around like a fuzzy old cat,
While the leaves gossip playfully, where they are at.
With twirls and with giggles, they whisper and tease,
In this funky little corner, they're living with ease.

A shadow, a flutter, a bonnie disguise,
The plants throw a party beneath glowing skies.
They chat with the shadows, they wiggle and sway,
Plotting out pranks for the night and the day.

So here's to the laughter, the warmth and the cheer,
In this leafy gathering, there's nothing to fear.
With a toast to the flames, and to nature's fine art,
We'll revel together, let the fun never part.

Fronds and Flames: A Serene Rapture

The flicker of flames, oh what a grand sight,
As the greens play the game of a leaf-styled fright.
They shimmy and shake, oh, what crafty delight,
In the dance of the shadows, they put up a fight.

With laughter like crackles, the glow warms the room,
As whispers from greens chase away all the gloom.
They mock the old logs with a leafy parade,
Making fun of their creaks, oh how they have strayed!

The blanket of coziness, laughter it spawns,
Dancing along in the night until dawn.
The flickers are friendly, and oh what a show,
As the fronds weave their stories, they steal the warm glow.

So here's to good times by the hearth all aglow,
With nature's companions, we feel the fun flow.
For in the warm glow, with laughter and grace,
The fronds share your secrets in that cozy space.

Flickers of Comfort in the Leafy Depths

In corners of warmth, where the shadows collide,
The leafy friends gather, with giggles they bide.
A flicker, a shuffle, oh what are they up to?
With each playful rustle, they share jokes anew.

With flames casting stories in dappled display,
The greens throw a bash that we can't look away.
Whispers bloom laughter, they conjure up joy,
Making mischief like kids with a brand new toy.

Around the warm hearth, where the good vibes align,
They hug and they clamor for a pinch of red wine.
"Who will take a sip? Raise your frond to the skies!"
They toast to the fire, with winks and bright sighs.

Oh, the essence of comfort in swirling green hues,
As nature reminds us of all the fun news.
In this leafy cabaret, they shine so bright,
In the warmth of the flickers, hearts dance with delight.

Hearthside Serenity in Nature's Twist

Beside the warm hearth, where the laughter is free,
The greens wiggle gently, oh what joy to see!
They stretch and they curl, with a wink in their eyes,
In this playful abode, it's all fun and no lies.

The firelight dances, the fronds start to sway,
In chorus with flames, they put on a play.
"Who'll join in our fun? Come on, don't be shy!"
The leaves giggle softly, as shadows pass by.

With smiles in the air, there's a ripple of glee,
As secrets are shared, like a cup of warm tea.
Each rustle a chuckle, each flicker a grin,
In the heart of the night, let the laughter begin.

So here's to the moments spent wild and carefree,
With greens by the glow, let's raise a cup of tea.
In this cozy embrace, where humor takes flight,
We savor the warmth, all through the night.

Ferns Encircling the Glow

Around the flames they huddle tight,
With leaves that rustle, what a sight!
They gossip tales of garden woes,
While we all roast like marshmallow pros.

Their fronds are waving, a leafy dance,
In unison, they take a chance.
"Who's the brightest?" one leaf quips,
As sparks fly high from our cozy slips.

The heat makes them sprawl and sway,
While we munch snacks in disarray.
The jokes they crack, a funny lot,
One sneezes! Oops! Now we're all caught.

So here we laugh, what a charade,
With leafy friends, we feel elated.
In this warm corner, life's a blast,
With giggles echoing, warmly cast.

Cozy Groves in the Hearth's Embrace

In the hearth's glow, the green ones smile,
Telling stories with leafy guile.
"Did you hear the one about the pot?"
They quiver and giggle, what a lot!

The flames crackle, they reach for more,
Whispering secrets, oh, what a chore!
"I've heard it's hot here, that's for sure!"
They tease each other, and then they pour.

With every flicker, a tale unfolds,
Of wild adventures in the bold.
"Bet I could outshine you with pizazz!"
Snickers arise, as green fronds jazz.

In this warm nook where laughter sticks,
The plants conspire, making their picks.
Watch out, dear guests, for leafy charm,
They're slyly plotting some cozy harm!

Green Whispers Amidst the Heat

In the warmth, the greens exchange a glance,
One shouts, "Let's have a leafy dance!"
With wobbly fronds, they start to sway,
While the humans munch, distracted—hey!

A frond spills tea, now that's a joke,
"Caution! We might just go up in smoke!"
The audience gasps, is it too late?
As laughter erupts, they seal their fate.

They share a chuckle over toasty tips,
While we snack on nachos and popcorn dips.
"Admit it, we're the real stars here!"
They shout above the crackling cheer.

So here we are, amidst the fun,
With leafy pals, we've just begun.
In their green embrace, we find delight,
As laughter dances into the night.

Shadows of Ferns by Warmth's Canvas

In the shadows, the greens convene,
Creating mischief, oh so keen.
"Let's start a riot!" one leaf suggests,
While we relax, they plot their quests.

Around the flicker, they take their stance,
Meeting up for a leafy prance.
"Who made the fire? What a joke!"
They quirk and giggle, in leafy cloak.

With hints of spice and cheesy puns,
They crack up, and the fun just runs.
"Did you hear about the plant that flew?"
Their laughter echoes, quite the crew!

So grab a snack and join the throng,
Where fronds and friends together belong.
In this warm hug, bad jokes are born,
With shadows dancing till the morn!

Hearthside Reflections

In the warm glow where shadows dance,
A frond attempts a wobbly prance.
It sways and spins, a leafish show,
Whispering tales of life's bravado.

The cat's confused, it tilts its head,
Is that a plant, or dreams instead?
As giggles rise, it takes a leap,
Into the brush, it dives so deep.

A sock escapes, a slipper flies,
Nature's antics beneath the skies.
The crackle, pop of the cozy heat,
While leafy comrades dance on feet.

"Keep it down!" I jest with glee,
"Not all can hold such jubilee!"
They wave their fronds, a giggling crowd,
As laughter spills, ever so loud.

The Comfort of Unfurling Fronds

A leafy friend took my best spot,
Curled up on cushions, oh what a plot!
It stretches wide, its tactics sly,
A pajama thief, oh how it'll try.

With roots and laughs entangled tight,
It hosts no party, yet feels so right.
The whispers float, a chatty breeze,
"Just move aside, I've earned my keys!"

As I sip tea, it rolls and flops,
While the kettle hums, my joy just pops.
What's this? A vine takes a bow?
"More room, please!"—it mocks my vow!

Leaves play poker in comical stance,
With acorns betting on the last dance.
In this chaos, all feels just fine,
I chuckle and think, "This life is divine!"

Quiet Nights with Nature's Touch

In corners where the shadows creep,
Lies a green friend, not one to sleep.
With a rustle soft, it shares a joke,
Under the mantle, it starts to poke.

The clock ticks slow, yet time takes flight,
As humor spills in the soft moonlight.
"Can you believe? I'm catching dust!"
It cackles loud, "Oh, that's a must!"

With each flicker, shadows play,
"Our buddies thrive in such dismay!"
A mismatched sock does a jig nearby,
While the plants laugh and sigh.

As solitude wraps me in its hug,
Even the pot looks quite snug.
In warmth, we dance, no need for more,
A quirky crew, whom I do adore!

Green Keepers of the Glow

In a patch of light, they gather round,
With leafy tales that know no bound.
"Why do we bloom when nights are long?"
They smile wide, "A hearty song!"

A rogue twig takes the solo part,
As ferny friends all play the heart.
With banter wild, they stretch and flex,
The night unfolds with leafy specs.

"Who made this mess? It wasn't me!"
A sprout exclaims with feigned decree.
"Just check my roots, they sing so sweet!"
Yet giggles burst, can't hide retreat.

In cozy nooks, their laughter flows,
Echoing love that gently grows.
With warmth and jest, they deck the night,
A green ensemble, a pure delight!

Nature's Heartbeat in Ember's Light

In the corner, the plants do sway,
Dancing to the warmth of the day.
Little leaves with a curious grin,
Whispering tales of where they've been.

Here in the glow, they'll stretch and twine,
While socks are stuck outside the line.
A lizard peeks from its cozy retreat,
Wondering why humans have cold feet.

The crackling sounds mix with the breeze,
As plants pretend they're fancy trees.
But we know their secrets, snug and shy,
They dream in green and reach for the sky.

So raise your glass to the leafy crew,
Who share the warmth and the laughter too.
In this hearth where nature has its say,
Let's celebrate in our silly way.

The Essence of Tranquility in Flames

A lazy cat sprawls, quite the sight,
Purring softly as day turns to night.
Beneath the logs, a worm sneaks past,
Wondering how long this fire will last.

The plants gossip in whispers low,
As wood crackles with a warm glow.
A marshmallow flew right through the air,
Landing on a leafy friend in despair.

Oh, the drama of summer's jest,
As critters scheme for their cozy nest.
With laughter bubbling in the light,
We toast to the warmth, oh what a night!

Each flicker tells a silly tale,
Of adventures in the trees and trails.
So let's not fret when things go wrong,
For nature dances in this silly song.

A Cozy Embrace of the Woodlands

Amidst the glow of merriment bright,
The woodland critters take to flight.
A squirrel, plump and full of cheer,
Makes a dash for the snack right near.

Eager vines stretch with glee and grace,
As shadows play in this cozy space.
A mouse sneezes, causing a stir,
And the night fills with a soft absurd.

Oh the joy of a marshy night,
With crickets joining the leafy fight.
They chirp a tune to the flickering flame,
While branches dance without a shame.

Let's laugh and sing by this glowing light,
With nature's heartbeat feeling just right.
For friends in green, both shy and bold,
Bring humor to our tales of old.

Stories Told in Flickers and Green

In the fire's glow, stories unfold,
While shadows leap, both shy and bold.
A beetle boasts of daring deeds,
While twigs roll their eyes at the sheer greed.

Flickering flames and rustling leaves,
The plant gossipers, in between heaves.
Chasing the glow, a fox trots sly,
Thinking it's known for its fashion high.

A cup of tea spills all with glee,
As nature giggles, wild and free.
Beneath the stars, so bright and brave,
We toast to the laughs that the night gave.

As tales weave through the fragrant air,
Each chuckle dances without a care.
In this cozy room, our hearts align,
With every flicker, oh how we shine!

Hearthside Harmony

In the glow of the crackling light,
A leafy friend takes flight,
It jiggles and sways with delight,
Mocking shadows, oh what a sight!

Chasing sparks with leafy glee,
Whispers of laughter, wild and free,
As if the ferns had the key,
To a dance that only they see!

Socks and slippers, they slip and slide,
While leafy pals in the corner hide,
The warmth pulls all in the tide,
An evergreen gathering, side by side.

So let us toast to the funky fronds,
Who giggle and tease with little absconds,
In this hearth where the fun responds,
To warmth, laughter, and heartfelt bonds.

The Dance of Shadows and Fronds

The shadows leap like goofy fools,
Around the room, they break all the rules,
While ferns join in with curling curls,
Dancing alongside the laughing girls!

Mismatched socks become the trend,
As fronds high-five everyone, my friend,
All who enter must twist and bend,
To the rhythm that the fireplace sends!

The cat looks on with disdainful grace,
As ferns chuckle in this wild space,
"Just don't forget your dance face!"
They giggle and tumble without a trace.

But as the night folds into dreams,
Leafy winks and bright beams,
Who knew such fun hid in the seams,
Of hearthside tales and fidgeting teams?

Warmth Amongst the Undergrowth

Amidst the snuggly blanket pile,
Funky foliage flaunts its style,
With curls and twirls that beguile,
A hilarious scene, just pause a while.

The coffee pot is boiling and hot,
Leaves chatter loudly, they plot a lot,
"Let's have a soirée, give it a shot!"
And soon the whole house becomes a spot!

Pillows bounce with a cushy thud,
As fronds engage in silly mud,
Beneath it all, a giggly flood,
Of laughter shared in the hearthside bud.

So when the evening draws near,
Join the leafy rollicking cheer,
For warmth among the friends we hold dear,
Is nothing short of a comedic sphere!

Secret Worlds beneath the Mantle

Beneath the mantle, secrets peek,
Where whispers of ferns play hide and seek,
Each little leaf, a silly sneak,
In this cozy nook, they start to speak!

"Did you hear the one about the flame?
A shy little log, who sought more fame?
It laughed so hard, it lost its name,
And now it's just known as 'the same'!"

The crackles join in with fiery zest,
Encouraging antics, a leafy fest,
"Bring on the laughter, let it invest,
In comedy, warmth, and fun at best!"

So gather 'round this quirky scene,
Where ferns and flames plot and preen,
In secret worlds, they reign supreme,
With laughter woven into the dream!

Fern Fragrance in the Evening Air

In the corner, a plant sits proud,
Smelling fresh, like a mossy cloud.
Stealing glances from the bowl,
It tickles noses, with leafy scrolls.

The couch is full of tangled limbs,
While the fern waves and softly grins.
It sways like it's got the moves,
With every laugh, the fire approves.

Grandma thinks it guards the space,
But it's just planning its escape race.
"Not too close!" she tells the cat,
While the fern plots under the hat.

When the flames flicker, shadows bend,
The plant's a jester, playing pretend.
"Maybe tonight, I'll host a ball,
Just me, the flames, and the cat named Paul."

Flickering Green in the Twilight

The lights are dim, the shadows creep,
I swear that plant is into deep sleep.
Yet somehow it jiggles with zest,
Dreaming of dancing, it must be blessed.

My friends appear, all eyes aglow,
"Did that leaf just wave? No way, no!"
We giggle as it sways with glee,
A spectacle of green, wild and free.

The leaves wiggle, a wacky act,
Competing with fire for attention, intact.
"Make way for the flora!" one friend does shout,
But the tickets are sold, there's no getting out.

As laughter echoes, the plant takes a bow,
With every chuckle, we all go "Wow!"
In the glow of warmth, we find our cheer,
In the antics of green, our worries disappear.

A Sanctuary of Warmth and Greenery

In this cozy nook where friends unite,
The greenery stirs in soft twilight.
It's more than foliage, it's a show,
With every snicker, it starts to glow.

Mugs uplifted, the jokes flow free,
While the leafy one joins the spree.
"Do you call this a houseplant affair?"
It seems to chuckle, "I'm beyond rare!"

It fluffs its leaves, gives a little cheer,
Some thought it died, now look at it here!
"Remember that time you forgot to water?"
It laughs, "I can thrive as a great plotter!"

Amidst the tales of mishaps and cheer,
That plant's the star, let's give a cheer!
In warmth and laughter, we must agree,
It's the funniest thing this plant could be.

Leaves That Danced with Fireflies

As twilight falls, the critters hum,
The plant joins in, it's quite the fun.
"C'mon now, let's get in the groove,"
Beneath the stars, it starts to move.

A gathering of friends, gleeful and bright,
Watching the leaves as they take flight.
"Do they think they're the stars of the show?"
"Why not!?" it whispers, "Let's put on a show!"

The wind assists, a gentle sway,
Twinkling lights join in the play.
"Since when do plants get to have fun?"
"From now on, pal, till the night is done!"

Giggles and gasps fill the lively air,
As the leaves twirl like they haven't a care.
"Let's dance all night, till the morning sun!"
With fireflies buzzing, the party won.

Fronds Awash in Warm Light

In the corner, a plant does sway,
As if it's dancing in dismay.
A leaf turned left, then right with glee,
Shouting, 'Look at me! I'm fancy-free!'

Beneath the glow, it leans and bends,
Pretending to chat with all its friends.
The cat walks by, it gives a wave,
This leafy crowd is mischief's rave!

They whisper jokes of sunlit days,
And serve up laughs in leafy ways.
Oh, to be a frond so bold,
In warmth of light, their stories told!

When winter bites and frosts do bite,
These greens still laugh, oh what a sight!
They giggle loud at human plight,
For what's a chill to their delight!

Nature's Tapestry at Twilight

In the twilight, greens conspire,
To ignite a warming fire.
With every snap and crackle cheer,
They share their truths, as night draws near.

A sprig sings out, 'I'm on a roll!'
'Last week I rooted; now I stroll!'
The laughter swells as shadows blend,
A jest amidst the dusk, my friend.

The starlit glow, the leaves confess,
'This isn't winter, it's a dress!'
They twirl around, their fibers gleam,
In nature's quilt, they chase a dream!

While humans bring their winter woes,
These greens just giggle as time flows.
Wrapped in mirth, they ride the night,
Nature's rebels, bold and bright!

Hearth Blossoms in the Winter Chill

By the hearth where the warmth does spill,
A gathering of leaves, what a thrill!
With every flutter and rustle loud,
They craft a party, small and proud.

A leaf with flair shouts, 'Who's got jokes?'
While others sway as they poke fun at folks.
With winter's chill, they've got the knack,
For turning frowns to smiles, no lack!

They sip on air as if it's tea,
And play a tune, both wild and free.
In the cozy nook, they twinkle bright,
Hearthside jesters, igniting the night!

So when you're cold and feeling gray,
Just check the plants—they'll save the day!
Their frolic helps the frost retreat,
While winter's party's now complete!

Glowing Embers, Wild Serenity

Amidst the glow where embers dance,
A leafy crew begins to prance.
With joyful sways and laughs so clear,
They toast to warmth as winter nears.

A frond yells out, 'Grab your hats!'
Join in the fun, no time for spats!
They pluck a tune from cracked old walls,
In wild serenity, humor calls.

They whisper tales of summer's plight,
Of sun and skies, and warm night's light.
Paired with embers, they strike a chord,
In this wild jest, all hearts are stored.

So come and join this leafy play,
Where warmth and fun just lead the way.
In laughter's echo, woes decay,
These greens ensure you'll dance today!

www.ingramcontent.com/pod-product-compliance
Lightning Source LLC
Chambersburg PA
CBHW070333120526
44590CB00017B/2863